EINSTEIN: A pictorial biography

"The discovery of nuclear chain reaction need not bring about the destruction of mankind any more than did the discovery of matches. . . . To have security against atomic bombs . . . we have to prevent war."

—ALBERT EINSTEIN

EINSTEIN

A pictorial biography

by WILLIAM CAHN

New York   THE CITADEL PRESS

Cover photograph by Fred Stein
Cover design by Lili Cassel

Second Printing

INTRODUCTION

What was there about Albert Einstein that distinguished him from many other great men of science?

History is replete with men of genius who responded to the needs of their time . . . who built upon the contributions of others . . . and added something of their own to the onward progress of man.

What distinguished Einstein from these?

As the following pages seek to show, Albert Einstein was more than a scientist, although, had he been that and nothing more, his name would still rank high in the annals of history.

Einstein was also an artist, always sensitive to the world of beauty around him. Einstein was a man of great social conscience, with—as he put it so well—"a passionate sense of social justice and social responsibility."

Einstein was a democrat, a man who had a devout respect for mankind. He was a man of peace who viewed war with contempt, as an enemy of everything he cherished.

Einstein was a man of his own people, the Jewish people. But his concern for the rights of all people made him a champion of the oppressed throughout his life.

These are some of the characteristics which distinguished Einstein from other men of science through the ages.

Many words will be written about Einstein. Many have already appeared. But, in some respects, words alone are inadequate in dealing with this man. Something of the firmament—which occupied so much of his time and study—reflected itself in him. He belonged to the universe . . . as a farmer belongs to the soil. Perhaps this is what won him such a warm place in the hearts of the common people of all lands.

This is why a *pictorial* biography of Albert Einstein appears so fitting. You may read his life in his eyes as well as in his words.

WILLIAM CAHN

There are a great many names in the history of
human progress . . .

Pythagoras studied the heavens
and the movements of planets . . .

Copernicus demonstrated

that the earth moves

around the sun . . .

8

Newton discovered the laws of gravitation . . .

Faraday invented the dynamo . . .

But none is greater than that of *Albert Einstein* . . . scientist . . . lover of mankind . . . citizen of the world . . . *a man who—in the words of Lord Haldane—"has called forth a greater revolution in thought than even Copernicus, Galileo, or Newton himself."*

It was his scientific theory, delivered to the world in 1905, that ushered in the atomic age.

Einstein's father.

Einstein's mother.

When a boy child was born to Hermann and Pauline Einstein on March 14, 1879, in the city of Ulm, Bavaria, there was no reason to suspect he would be one of the world's great men. The Einsteins were hard put financially to raise their two children, Albert and his younger sister Maja. Both children developed normally, although the parents noted that Albert was slow to talk and slower to read. . . .

14

Young Albert and his sister Maja.

"Teachers in the elementary school," recalled Einstein in later years," appeared to me like sergeants. . . ." ▶

In school Albert had his troubles. This was the era of the iron-handed ruler of Germany—*Bismarck*. Militarism and intolerance crept into all phases of life in Munich, where the Einsteins had moved. In the schools, this meant rigid discipline for the children . . . absolute obedience . . . no questioning.

16

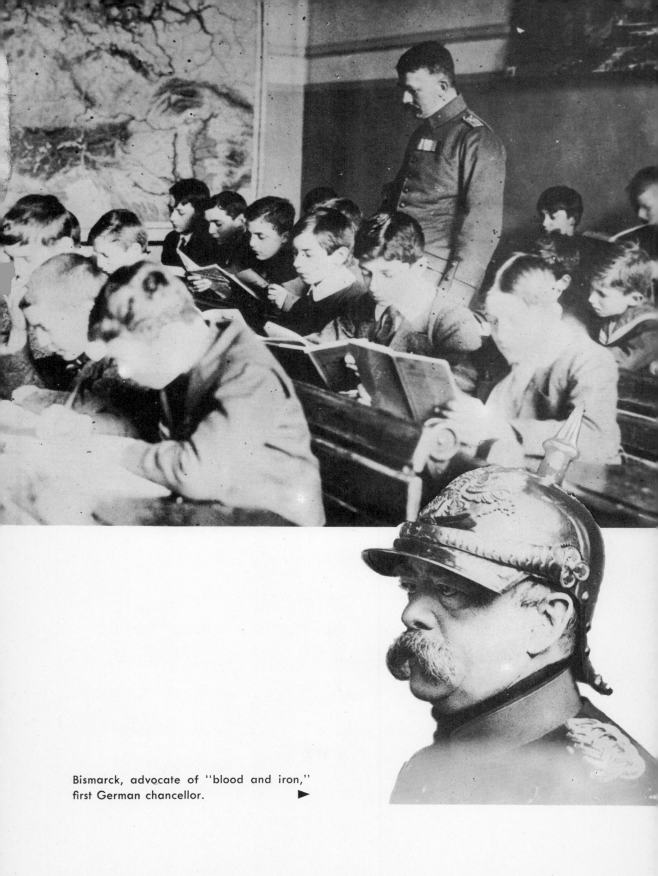

Bismarck, advocate of "blood and iron," first German chancellor. ▶

In preference to his school studies, Einstein turned to the study of the heavens. "Out yonder," he said, "there was this huge world, which exists independently of us human beings. . . . The contemplation of this world beckons like a liberation." ▶

From his earliest years, young Einstein had, as he put it, a *"furious impulse to understand, to be informed . . ."* But the dry-as-dust teachings in the schools bored him. Albert turned eagerly to the more sympathetic instruction of an elderly uncle at home. The uncle introduced him to the science of mathematics: *"It is a merry science . . . When the animal that we are hunting cannot be caught, we call it X temporarily and continue to hunt it until it is bagged."*

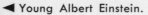

◀ Young Albert Einstein.

When his parents moved, Albert welcomed the chance to transfer his schooling to Switzerland . . . a land free from German militarism. Soon he had settled down to an intensive mathematical training. When the opportunity presented itself, he renounced his German status and became a citizen of Switzerland.

Famous Declaration of Independence of Switzerland, dating back to 1291.

Albert Einstein and his wife, Mileva.

After graduating from the Swiss Federal Polytechnic school in 1896 at Zurich, Einstein set out to look for employment as a teacher. He was convinced that his interests lay in the field of mathematics and science. But jobs were scarce. He finally was forced to accept one as a clerk in the patent office at Berne. The job paid little. But he needed the work because he was married now, to a fellow student, Mileva Maritsch, a young Serbian woman. Two sons were soon born to them.

Berne, Switzerland, where Einstein found his first job.

Fortunately, Einstein's job as a patent clerk permitted him spare time for his own scientific work. Albert needed the time. Problems in theoretical physics—seeking to understand the make-up of the universe—challenged him. It was a time ripe for re-examining the theories of Newton, which needed to be brought up to date. Because Einstein refused to accept any theory uncritically . . . because he insisted on examining the superstitions and prejudices of his day in the world of science . . . he was uniquely equipped to extend the horizon of man's knowledge like no one else of his century.

Sir Isaac Newton ▲

Albert Einstein ▶

Who could have guessed that an article by an unknown patent office clerk, appearing in the German scientific journal, *Annalen der Physik,* volume 17, in the year 1905, would turn the world of science topsy-turvy? But that is what was to occur.

In this and other such articles, Einstein showed the inter-relationship of time, space and matter. In his Theory of Relativity, Einstein showed that matter is actually concentrated energy. From this he put forward the most famous mathematical formula ever projected:

This formula states, in the shorthand of physics, that the energy contained in any particle of matter is equal to the mass of that matter multiplied by the speed of light (186,000 miles a second), and again multiplied by the speed of light.

ANNALEN

DER

PHYSIK.

BEGRÜNDET UND FORTGEFÜHRT DURCH

F. A. C. GREN, L. W. GILBERT, J. C. POGGENDORFF, G. UND E. WIEDEMANN.

VIERTE FOLGE.

BAND 17.

DER GANZEN REIHE 322. BAND.

KURATORIUM:

F. KOHLRAUSCH, M. PLANCK, G. QUINCKE,
W. C. RÖNTGEN, E. WARBURG.

DER DEUTSCHEN P

UN

H

PAU

MIT F

VERLAG VON

5. *Über die von der molekularkinetischen Theorie der Wärme geforderte Bewegung von in ruhenden Flüssigkeiten suspendierten Teilchen;*
von A. Einstein.

In dieser Arbeit soll gezeigt werden, daß nach der molekularkinetischen Theorie der Wärme in Flüssigkeiten suspendierte Körper von mikroskopisch sichtbarer Größe infolge der Molekularbewegung der Wärme Bewegungen von solcher Größe ausführen müssen, daß diese Bewegungen leicht mit dem Mikroskop nachgewiesen werden können. Es ist möglich, daß die hier zu behandelnden Bewegungen mit der sogenannten „Brown schen Molekularbewegung" identisch sind; die mir erreichbaren Angaben über letztere sind jedoch so ungenau, daß ich mir hierüber kein Urteil bilden konnte.

Wenn sich die hier zu behandelnde Bewegung samt den für sie zu erwartenden Gesetzmäßigkeiten wirklich beobachten läßt, so ist die klassische Thermodynamik schon für mikroskopisch unterscheidbare Räume nicht mehr als genau gültig anzusehen und es ist dann eine exakte Bestimmung der wahren Atomgröße möglich. Erwiese sich umgekehrt die Voraussage dieser Bewegung als unzutreffend, so wäre damit ein schwerwiegendes Argument gegen die molekularkinetische Auffassung der Wärme gegeben.

§ 1. Über den suspendierten Teilchen zuzuschreibenden osmotischen Druck.

Im Teilvolumen V^* einer Flüssigkeit vom Gesamtvolumen V seien z-Gramm-Moleküle   Ist
das Volumen   für die ge

At first Einstein's Theory did not make a ripple. Then a few of the leading scientists took notice. Soon the entire scientific world was discussing it. Einstein showed that the use of atomic energy is theoretically possible. But no one knew whether or not it could actually happen. *"It takes one's breath away,"* wrote Prof. J. H. Thirring of the University of Vienna at the time, *"to think of what might happen in a town, if the dormant energy of a single brick were to be set free, say in the form of an explosion. . . . This, however, will never happen. . . ."*

Forty years later, in a blinding flash at Hiroshima, such an opinion was to be proven wrong. . . .

Meanwhile Einstein, a youth of 26, already showed the combination of gentle irony and humor which was to mark his outlook on life throughout his years. *"If my theory is proven correct,"* Einstein remarked, *"Germany will hail me as a great German, and the French will hail me as a citizen of the world. If it is proven false, the French will call me a German and the Germans will call me a Jew."*

Albert Einstein's reputation now spread far beyond Europe. He became a world figure, as Sir J. J. Thomson, respected English research physicist stated, for *"one of the greatest achievements in the history of human thought."* Invitations to lecture or teach came from many universities. In 1909 Einstein felt he could give up his patent office job, and he accepted a university teaching post in Switzerland. In 1913 he was invited by Kaiser Wilhelm II to come back to Germany to become director of the newly created Kaiser Wilhelm Institute in Berlin. Although Einstein had no desire to return to Germany, the position offered him the opportunity to do his scientific work without hindrance of any kind. And so he accepted the offer.

Professor Einstein speaking
before an attentive audience
of distinguished scientists in
Berlin.

On his return to Germany, Einstein was warmly welcomed by his former friends and relatives. Among these was his cousin, Elsa Einstein, a childhood companion who—like Einstein himself—had married early in life, had two children, and was now divorced. Einstein had not found happiness in his home life and had separated from his wife who remained in Switzerland with their two sons. The two cousins—Albert and Elsa—became inseparable and, a few years after his return to Germany, they were married. Mrs. Einstein was a friendly, devoted woman, more interested in creating a pleasant home than in her husband's scientific accomplishments. *"My interest in mathematics,"* she once said, *"is mainly in the household bills."*

A world figure, Einstein early became a patient target for photographers.

Einstein had scarcely returned to Germany when war between the German Empire and England, Russia and France broke out. Since childhood, Einstein had hated militarism and war. Now he tried to ignore the wave of military fervor that swept the nation. But it was impossible. Soon Einstein became known as a pacifist. *"I had rather be smitten to shreds than participate in such doings,"* he said. When leading German fellow scientists upheld Germany's part in the war which was engulfing the entire world, Einstein condemned their action, termed the war *"senseless violence."* Only his world renown saved Einstein from persecution by the German state.

At last the war ended. What Einstein described as a *"mean, contemptible thing"* was over. And now his scientific accomplishments marked him a world celebrity. A modern successor to Copernicus and Newton, he captured the popular imagination. Thousands of "explanations" of the Einstein Theory were printed. . . . Moving pictures were made explaining it. . . . The theory became a favorite subject for lectures and debates. . . . Einstein himself became a household word in nations throughout the world. . . . Children whom he never would see were named after him. . . . He was invited to contribute articles to popular magazines . . . to give speeches before ladies' clubs . . . to provide his autograph. A tobacco manufacturer named a cigar after him. He was one of the most famous of the German people.

Einstein at a dinner with George Bernard Shaw, at extreme right. In the center is Lord Rothschild.

Speaking of great world figures, George Bernard Shaw, the playwright, said: *"Napoleon and other great men were makers of empires, but these men whom I am about to mention were makers of universes, and their hands were not stained with the blood of their fellow men. I go back 2,500 years and how many can I count in that period? I can count them on the fingers of my two hands. Pythagoras, Ptolemy, Kepler, Copernicus, Aristotle, Galileo, Newton and Einstein."*

Albert Einstein and Rabindranath Tagore, famous Indian poet.

Einstein had now developed into sturdy, robust maturity. Careless of his dress, impatient with the small deceits and talk of the social world about him, Einstein's independence grew with passing years. Ever ready—even eager—to give time and attention to those who really needed it, he refused to waste a moment with those who merely sought him out as a celebrity . . . a world figure. Modesty, in the face of rapidly growing fame, was also a characteristic: *"It is an irony of fate that I myself have been the recipient of excessive admiration and reverence from my fellow beings, through no fault and no merit of my own. . . ."* Despite his position, he refused to alter his simple habits and manner of living. Money did not appear to interest him. *"I refuse to make money out of my science,"* he said. *"My laurel is not for sale. . . ."*

Einstein became impatient with the idea, commonly held, that his theory was so difficult that only ten men in the world are capable of comprehending it. *"Every earnest student of theoretical physics,"* he maintained, *"is in a position to comprehend it."*

40

Einstein and a student
at Princeton. ▶

Einstein never permitted his deep interest in science to shut him off from the daily interests of the world about him. His support for Palestine, a homeland for the Jews, was an example of this. Although Einstein had been brought up as a free thinker and without orthodox background, he became convinced of the importance of Palestine. Noting the rise of anti-Semitism in post-war Germany, Einstein said: *"If we did not have to live among intolerant, narrow-minded and violent people, I should be the first to throw over all nationalism."*

But, largely as a result of his growing experience with anti-Semitism, Einstein—the man who hated nationalism—agreed in mid-life on the importance of the Zionist movement.

◄ Einstein with Dr. Chaim Weizmann, British scientist and leader of the Zionist movement, who did much to interest Einstein in Palestine.

With increased energy, Einstein devoted precious time to the movement to raise funds for a Jewish homeland. *"It is not enough for us to play a part as individuals,"* he said, *"We must also tackle tasks which only nations as a whole can perform."* When the proposal was made that Dr. Weizmann and Einstein visit America to raise funds for Palestine, especially the Hebrew University there, Einstein agreed. In April, 1921, Einstein and his wife, Dr. Weizmann and party arrived in America.

Although the ship was hours late, a special reception committee waited patiently. It included New York's Mayor Hylan; Alfred E. Smith, soon to be elected Governor of New York; Arthur Brisbane, journalist; Judge Ben Cardozo; Fiorello La-Guardia, president of the City Council; and Mrs. William Randolph Hearst.

44

EINSTEIN, IN CLEVELAND EXPLAINS THEORY

The reception given Albert Einstein in the United States was unprecedented. Never had a scientist been the subject of such interest. Thousands waited on the streets to cheer him in New York . . . Cleveland . . . Pittsburgh. Thousands were turned away at meetings where he appeared. In Cleveland, storekeepers closed up at noon to take part in a giant parade in his honor. In Washington, he was personally received by President Harding.

Dr. Einstein being welcomed to New York.

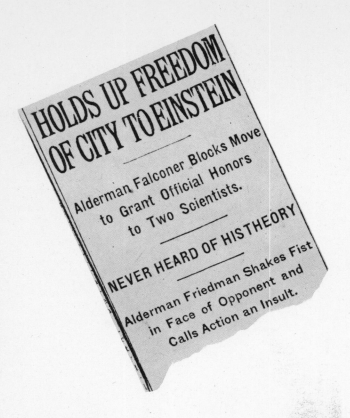

HOLDS UP FREEDOM OF CITY TO EINSTEIN

Alderman Falconer Blocks Move to Grant Official Honors to Two Scientists.

NEVER HEARD OF HIS THEORY

Alderman Friedman Shakes Fist in Face of Opponent and Calls Action an Insult.

But all was not sweetness and light. Some American publications questioned Einstein's accuracy and called his theory *"worthless and misleading."* A group of women from a "patriotic" organization demanded that Einstein be refused entrance to the country because of his *"communistic"* ideas. Hearing of this, Nicholas Murray Butler, president of Columbia University, declared himself *"humiliated and disgraced."* New York's City Council became a center of angry controversy when one member objected to offering Einstein the key to the city, claiming he had never heard of Einstein's theory.

IS EINSTEIN'S ARITHMETIC OFF?

DOES A TRIVIAL ARITHMETICAL ERROR, the omission of a simple numerical factor, vitiate Professor Einstein's calculations of the sun's gravitational effect on the light ray from a star? ...
said to substa...
confirm that ...
somewhat surp...
in a public add...
emy of Scien...
plete triumph ...
universal grav...
See, professor ...
Navy, and gov...
Island. Profes...
plained the p...
which he says...
after ...
Weyl, ...
other ...
utterly ...
most p...
age." ...
wired fr...
Times.

"It s...
Newton...
plained ...
satellite...
centurie...
determin...
only hal...
light pa...
total ecl...
"On ...
tency, t...
the imp...
error of ...
the mat...
lowers h...
mathem...
and I a...
modern ...
think it ...
By persi...
special fi...
to learn ...
disciple o...

Profess...

"It wa...
traveling ...
just grazing the ...
center by .84 of a...
discovery of phot...
flection could be ...
not double his ca...
the sun to be obs...
"In 1911 Eins...
a slightly differe...
law of wh... that used in 1801, getting...
actly Soldner's f... numerical value, .84 second of arc...
In 1916 Einstein doubled his value, making it 1.68 or 1.7 second...
for rays observed upon the earth, yet he could explain only half
of this amount by the Newtonian theory of gravitation. For he
made an error of calculation by which, when the ray had passed
the sun to the earth, he still got only .84 second of arc, as
Soldner had done in 1801 for a ray just coming up to the sun from

other half of the observed deflection, .84 second of arc, Einstein
explained by the doctrine of the 'Curvature of Space,' which is
now shown to be erroneous.

...n his calculation by an erroneous differential
bending of the path of the light. By careless...
...ted a multiplier, two, for the angle, and hence
when he integrated the expression to finish
his calculation of the bending of the ray, he
gets only half of the value required by correct physical mathematics.

"This error of Einstein was so securely
hidden that it escaped all the mathematicians
of Europe for the past thirteen years, and as
a great mass of literature on relativity now
exists, a very competent authority has assured
me that the error might have escaped notice
for another century but for the peculiar circumstances which made the discovery possible at Mare Island, California, on September 12, 1924.

"I set about constructing geometrically
the bending of the wave-front imagined in
the theory of relativity, and when I had
made a suitable and accurate figure, I was
able to show by simple geometry the error
in Einstein's original equation of 1911, which
has since continued to be repeated by
Richardson, Eddington and the other authorities on relativity, not one of them suspecting that all their work was vitiated by
an error which a high-school student can
now understand.

"As an outcome of this discovery, we now
have a correct method of calculating the
bending of the light, by the sun's gravita...
...tional attraction. We find that by the cor...

time upon time and has been found to be correct,' he said.

"'Of course, if any one should prove that there was a serious
error in the calculations or the theory, it would necessarily have

---

IS THE EINSTEIN THEORY A CRAZY VAGARY?

IT SURELY IS, according to Capt. T. J. J. See, of the
U. S. Navy, one of the astronomers who has refused to
bow the knee to Relativity. The recent eclipse observations agree not only with Einstein, he says, but with astronomical
formulas deduced over a century ago. Furthermore, Einstein's
theory of gravitation fails to explain familiar phenomena and is,
as above stated, "a crazy vagary" and "a disgrace to the age."
Professor See has himself promulgated a theory of gravitation,
which he says is not open to these or similar
... ...versions; but we quote him here only
... ...n to that proposed by Einstein.
... in a letter from California, printed
... ...w York *Times*:

...can not be truthfully said that the
...ion of the Newton-Soldner formula
...or the refraction of starlight near
...is a triumph for Einstein. This
...dates from the early days of Ein-
...andfather—122 years ago!—and in
...h from Berlin, April 14, Einstein
...dmitted to the correspondent, Karl
...and, that 'in so far as precise mea-
...is concerned Captain See may be
...e correct in de...
...he theory of re...
...owever, that ...
...ances the difficu...
...removed. It ...
...does not rega...
...riumphed, and a...
...mature.
...u admit the g...
...by eminent Eu...

...anuary of this ...
...rlin that fifty ...
...aticians and oth...
...ly grieved" to ...
...y the suggestio...
...y is the solutio...
...erse, and by th...
...many savants...
...this theory as...

...In the circumstances, is it any wonder
...owe a duty of truth to the public should
vigorously the unauthorized and indefen...
the observed refraction of starlight near the...
of the discredited doctrine of relativity?

"3. After ample reflection I have de...
'discredited,' and I will now r... ... giv...

"(a) Einstein's f...

A BEST MIND TACKLES THE EINSTEIN THEORY
—Kirby in the New York *World*.

"WORTHLESS, MISLEADING"

Is Einstein's theory of relativity,
says Captain T. J. J. See, because
it is all based on a mathematical
error "which a high school student
can now understand."

In Washington, both Houses of Congress found themselves caught up in the discussion sweeping America. Einstein's Theory of Relativity became the subject of Congressional attention with no Congressman claiming to understand it. . . .

Mr. PENROSE. Mr. President, will the Senator permit an inquiry?

Mr. WILLIAMS. Certainly.

Mr. PENROSE. The Senator has referred very eloquently to Newton and others who have contributed to science. I know the Senate would patiently listen to him if he would explain his views on Einstein's theory of relativity.

Mr. WILLIAMS. Mr. President, I have long contended that the wittiest, the vaguest, and most indefinite man in this body is the Senator from Pennsylvania, but I did not know until this morning that he could discover anything more vague and indefinite than himself. I frankly confess that I do not understand Einstein; I frankly confess that I do not believe the Senator from Pennsylvania understands Einstein; I frankly confess I do not believe the Senator from Connecticut [Mr. BRANDEGEE] would even contend that he understood Einstein, and I do not believe that even the Senator from Massachusetts [Mr. LODGE] would make a very positive pretense in that direction.

Mr. PENROSE. Mr. President——

The VICE PRESIDENT. Does the Senator from Mississippi yield to the Senator from Pennsylvania?

Mr. WILLIAMS. I yield.

Mr. PENROSE. I own a volume of Einstein, in the introduction of which it is stated that there are only 12 men in all the world who understand the book. I thought, perhaps, the Senator from Mississippi was one of them. I confess that I have nearly lost my mental faculties in trying to understand Einstein.

Mr. WILLIAMS. Mr. President, I believe it was the Earl of Derby who once said that there were only two men who ever understood the Near Eastern question, that one of them was dead and that he himself was getting old and had pretty nearly forgotten it all. [Laughter.] So far as Einstein is concerned, I did endeavor for a little while to try to understand Einstein; I do not believe the Senator from Pennsylvania ever even tried; but I frankly had the wisdom to confess that I did not understand Einstein. However, Mr. President, I do understand that there are certain great fundamental, cardinal principles of fairness which exist in the world, and I know that the Senator from Pennsylvania knows that, too.

The VICE PRESIDENT. The yeas and nays have been ordered on agreeing to the resolution, and the Secretary will call the roll.

The reading clerk proceeded to call the roll.

Mr. DILLINGHAM (when his name was called)... the same pair and transfer as on the last vote...

Mr. EDGE (when his name was... same pair and transfer as on the...

Mr. HARRIS (when his name... same transfer of my p...

Mr. McCUMBER... my pair as...

Mr. Mc... my...

Broussard	Hitchcock
Caraway	Jones, N. Mex.
Dial	McKellar
Fletcher	Overman
Harris	Pomerene
Harrison	Ransdell
Heflin	Reed

NOT V

Ashurst	Gerry
Borah	Glass
Calder	Gooding
Culberson	Johnson
Elkins	Kendrick
Fernald	King
Frelinghuysen	Knox

So Mr. BRANDEGEE'S

Mr. HARRISON. ... that the vote by whic... tion has passed does... that it requires a two... tion may pass. I d... in again discussi... I made when ... ago, I cited ... precedent in ... for the suspen... its adoption re...

The VICE ... motion is not ... and that it onl... therefore over...

Mr. LODGE. ... XXIV as provi... committees...

The V... so orde...

Mr. ... the d...

Th... offer... cons...

M...

M...

in...

Finally, after a highly successful and enthusiastic visit, Dr. and Mrs. Einstein and party said a grateful farewell to America and left for England and then home to Berlin. The last day in America was marked by a dinner at New York's Hotel Astor where 1,200 men and women greeted Einstein as not only a great scientist but also a *great Jew, the possessor of a warm and beautiful heart.*

Professor and Mrs. Einstein's farewell dinner in 1921. Seated, left to right, Felix M. Warburg, Professor and Mrs. Einstein. Standing, left to right, Robert Szold, President of the Zionist Organization of America; Morris Rothenberg, chairman of the American Palestine Campaign; Rabbi Stephen S. Wise and Jefferson Seligmann.

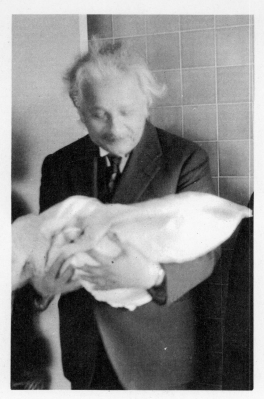

◄ Einstein and the baby of a friend, named after him.

When the Einsteins returned to Berlin, they found chaos. Germany, defeated in war, was torn by inner strife. Tens of thousands were unemployed. Einstein sought to bury himself in his work at the Kaiser Wilhelm Institute. Weather permitting, he would go for long sails in his beloved sail-boat. But the plight of people he saw everywhere could not be ignored. . . .

54

School children in Berlin, suffering from insufficient nourishment, grow tired quickly after a short period of play.

Moved by his *"passionate sense of social justice and social responsibility,"* Einstein found it impossible to ignore the condition of the people of Berlin. *"It is no easy matter for me,"* he admitted, *"to overcome my natural inclination to a life of quiet contemplation."* Einstein supported the idea, as a solution to the unemployment crisis, of a *"statutory reduction of working hours, graduated for each department of industry, in order to get rid of unemployment, combined with the fixing of minimum wages. . . ."*

Einstein found the world of political ideas intruding into his work. During the war his strong pacifism had earned him many enemies in the German state. Now, with misery on every hand, an attempt was made to find scapegoats to blame for the conditions that existed. The pacifists were excellent targets for blame . . . as were the democrats and the Jews . . . *And Einstein was all three!* In addition, he insisted on using his vast prestige to speak out in behalf of any cause which he believed was in the interest of democratic principles. . . . Independent and fiercely stubborn about what he believed was right, Einstein brushed aside attempts of his friends who cautioned him against his actions.

Einstein championed every cause he viewed as just. He appealed for amnesty for German labor and political prisoners. He read of the celebrated Tom Mooney case in the United States and addressed a letter to the Governor of California characterizing the sentencing of the American labor leader as *"a miscarriage of justice."* Similarly, he spoke out for fair treatment for the two Italian-Americans, Sacco and Vanzetti, and for the seven Negro youths known as the "Scottsboro Boys." Especially did he oppose attempts in his own country to dismiss from their jobs people holding liberal ideas. This he called a *"program of annihilation"* wherein *"the learned societies of Germany have . . . stood by and said nothing while . . . German students and professional men . . . have been deprived of all chances of getting employment. . . ."*

Einstein is shown testifying in defense of his friend, Professor Gumbel (third from the left) who had been attacked for his political views. Said Einstein, "Professor Gumbel's only offense has been to fight against political murder. . . . What is to become of a people who brutally harass such a contemporary?"

◄ Einstein identified himself closely with the Jewish community in Germany. Here he is shown playing the violin in a Berlin synagogue on the occasion of a charity concert in 1930.

It was no wonder that Einstein became a special target for enemies of German democracy. Einstein perceived the great menace of the Hitler movement and its doctrines of German "supermen" and "inferior races." *"Let every man be respected as an individual and no man idolized,"* Einstein said.

◀ Pastor Niemoeller, victim of Nazi brutality, is shown leaving Jesus Christ Church in Dahlem, Easter 1937, just before he was arrested and sent to a concentration camp for his opposition to the Nazis.

Raids on the Jewish community grew in ferocity. *"The sight made my heart bleed,"* Einstein wrote a friend. But it was not only the Jews that bore the brunt of the attack. All forces that opposed total destruction of democracy were attacked: Freemasons, Catholics, Protestants, trade unionists, Socialists.

"When the Germans had lost the World War hatched by the ruling class," said Einstein, *"immediate attempts were made to blame the Jews, first for instigating the war and then for losing it. . . . The hatred engendered against the Jews . . . protected the privileged classes. . . ."*

Nazi storm-troopers hold anti-Semitic signs calling for a boycott of Jewish merchants.

It didn't matter to the Nazis that, in 1932, Albert Einstein was awarded a Nobel prize. The prize money, $50,000, Einstein sent to his former wife and his two sons, living in Switzerland. Because of his international prominence, the Nazis feared Einstein and placed him on their list of "dangerous" people. Among the many inflammatory leaflets issued against Einstein was one with his picture and the words: *Not yet hanged!* When the Nazis openly burned books of "enemies of the state," Einstein's *Theory of Relativity* was included. Einstein's *Theory* was called "Bolshevistic physics" and an effort was made to drop the "Einstein" from the "Einstein Theory."

ANNALEN
DER
PHYSIK.

BEGRÜNDET UND FORTGEFÜHRT DURCH

F. A. C. GREN, L. W. GILBERT, J. C. POGGENDORFF, G. UND E. WIEDEMANN.

VIERTE FOLGE.

BAND 17.

DER GANZEN REIHE 322. BAND.

KURATORIUM:

F. KOHLRAUSCH, M. PLANCK, G. QUINCKE,
W. C. RÖNTGEN, E. WARBURG.

UNTER MITWIRKUNG

DER DEUTSCHEN PHYSIKALISCHEN GESELLSCHAFT

UND INSBESONDERE VON

M. PLANCK

HERAUSGEGEBEN VON

PAUL DRUD

MIT

Deutsche Studenten ... wider den undeutschen Geist

12238

The militarism that Einstein hated became the rule of Nazi Germany. The young . . . the old . . . *everybody marched.* . . .

Obviously, there was no place for Einstein in fascist Germany. Threats were made on his life. Young fascist youth burst into his classroom crying *"Drive the Jew out!"* For the first time, Einstein realized fully what it meant to be a Jew. *"And I owe this discovery more to gentiles than to Jews."*

"Safety is impossible here," he said in a newspaper interview. *"Detectives sleep on the stairs. There are secret service men in the grounds, and my wife is terribly worried."*

An emissary of the Central Belgian police bureau in Brussels is shown calling on Professor Einstein at his summer home at Coq-Sur-Mer, Belgium, to tell him that the police can no longer guarantee his safety from Nazi attack.

While Einstein was visiting friends in England, the news was announced that the Nazis had set a price on his head. Picture shows how Einstein's friends and his two secretaries took to arms to secure his safety. ▼

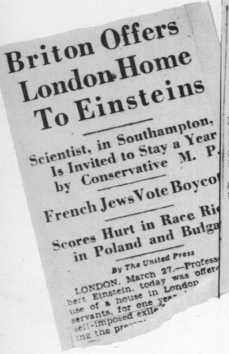

Briton Offers London Home To Einsteins

Scientist, in Southampton, Is Invited to Stay a Year by Conservative M. P.

French Jews Vote Boycot

Scores Hurt in Race Ri— in Poland and Bulga—

By The United Press

LONDON, March 27.—Profess— bert Einstein, today was offer— use of a house in London servants, for one yea— self-imposed exile— ing the pre—

BELGIAN HAVEN FOR EINSTEIN

ANTWERP, Belgium, Mar. 29.— Prof. Albert Einstein is going to stay in Belgium for five months, and will remain away from Germany, his home, if conditions like those prevalent today continue.

Arriving here aboard the Belgenland from the United States, the German savant said:

"I consider Germany a country with a 'sick psychology.' I will never return while this situation lasts.

"I intend to remain in Belgium more tha— staying at — Ostend — wh—

PROF. EINSTEIN GOING TO SPAIN

MADRID, April 10 (AP).—Prof. —lbert Einstein, who renounced —s German citizenship because of —ti-Semitism in Germany, today —ed an invitation to become —f the faculty of the —d.

—s. minister — the

Despite the personal efforts of King Albert of Belgium to guarantee the safety of Einstein, the danger to his life grew. In November, 1933, the Einstein family fled. When this news was made public, invitations of asylum were offered from many nations . . . England . . . France . . . the United States. . . . In an answer to Hitler's persecutions, Einstein declared: *"As long as I have any choice, I will stay only in a country where political liberty, toleration and equality of all citizens before the law are the rule. . . . Political liberty implies liberty to express one's political opinions orally or in writing, and a tolerant respect for any and every individual opinion. . . ."*

The Institute of Advanced Study, at Princeton, New Jersey, in the United States, had for some time been urging Einstein to join its staff. After careful consideration, he and Mrs. Einstein decided to make America their new home. The university proposed that Einstein set his own salary. Dr. Einstein indicated that he believed $3,000 a year would be ample.

"Could I live on less?" he asked a representative of the university.

"You couldn't live on that," he was told.

His salary was set at $16,000 a year. Soon the Einstein family was at home at 112 Mercer Street, Princeton, New Jersey.

The Einstein family, surrounded by relatives, as they prepared to leave for America. Left to right: Frau Dimitri Marianoff, a daughter; Dr. Marianoff, the latter's husband; Professor Einstein; friends and, extreme right, Mrs. Einstein.

NAZIS HUNT ARMS IN EINSTEIN HOME

Only a Bread Knife Rewards Brown Shirts' Search for Alleged Huge Cache.

OUSTING OF JEWS GOES ON

Physicians Are Removed From Hospitals and Judges From the Criminal Courts.

◄ Shortly after Einstein left Germany, a reward of 20,000 marks was placed on his head. "I didn't know I was worth so much," he said.

Professor and Mrs. Einstein relax in their new home at Princeton, New Jersey. ►

Away from the dread Nazi state, Einstein quickly adjusted himself to his work at Princeton. In addition to his independent research, the relaxed professor enjoyed his classes where he became a favorite of advanced Princeton students. Awed by his great fame, the young people would sometimes hesitate to bother Einstein with their problems. *"I shall always be able to receive you,"* he told them. *"If you have a problem, come to me with it. You will never disturb me, since I can interrupt my own work at any moment."*

76

Students sang this song about Einstein:

> The bright boys, they all study math
> And Albie Einstein points the path
> Although he seldom takes the air
> We wish to God he'd cut his hair.

Matching wit with wit, Einstein once gave this humorous answer to a request for a popular definition of relativity: *"When a man sits with a pretty girl for an hour, it seems to him a minute. But let him sit on a hot stove for only a minute—and it's longer than an hour. That's relativity."*

Famous Nobel prize winners pose for a picture. Left to right: Sinclair Lewis, Frank B. Kellogg, Einstein, and Irving Langmuir.

What impression did Einstein make on his colleagues? Perhaps the best answer was given by his close friend and associate for many years, Leopold Infield:

"One of my colleagues in Princeton asked me: 'If Einstein dislikes his fame and would like to increase his privacy, why does he not do what ordinary people do? Why does he wear his hair long, a funny leather jacket, no socks, no suspenders, no collars, no ties?'

"The answer is simple. The idea is to restrict his needs and, by this restriction, increase his freedom. We are slaves of millions of things. We are slaves of bathrobes, Frigidaires, cars, radios, and millions of other things. Einstein tried to reduce them to the absolute minimum. Long hair minimized the need for the barber. Socks can be done without. One leather jacket solves the coat problem for many years. Suspenders are superfluous, as are nightshirts and pajamas."

"The only thing that gives me pleasure, apart from my work, my violin and my sailboat, is the appreciation of my fellow workers."

◄ Einstein talks with Rabbi Stephen S. Wise and Thomas Mann, Nobel prize-winning author.

◄ Charlie Chaplin plays host to Einstein at a motion picture premiere.

◄ Conferring with Mayor Fiorello LaGuardia of New York.

On October 1, 1940, Albert Einstein took the oath of allegiance, becoming a citizen of the United States. On his right is his daughter, Margot. On his left is Miss Helen Dukas, his personal secretary.

"My life is a simple thing that would interest no one," stated Einstein. Yet on August 2, 1939 he was to take an action which would drastically alter the future of all mankind. . . .

When President Roosevelt received the letter from Einstein on the need for atomic research, he turned to his advisors saying, "This requires action." The result was the Manhattan Project. ▶

Shortly after his arrival in the United States in 1933, Einstein revealed the fact that he was no longer a pacifist: "*We must ever face battles when it becomes necessary to safeguard law and human dignity,*" he stated. "*Since the arrival of the fascist danger, I for the present no longer believe in the effectiveness of the absolute passive pacifism. As long as fascism rules in Europe, there will be no peace.*"

When Einstein heard that Hitler Germany was carrying forward experiments on nuclear fission which might lead to powerful new weapons, he knew that action was needed. *He wrote a letter to President Roosevelt. . . .*

Albert Einstein
Old Grove Rd.
Nassau Point
Peconic, Long Island

August 2nd, 1939

F.D. Roosevelt,
President of the United States,
White House
Washington, D.C.

Sir:

Some recent work by E.Fermi and L. Szilard, which has been com-
municated to me in manuscript, leads me to expect that the element uranium may be turned into a new and important source of energy in the immediate future. Certain aspects of the situation which has arisen seem
to call for watchfulness and, if necessary, quick action on the part
of the Administration. I believe therefore that it is my duty to bring
to your attention the following facts and recommendations:

In the course of the last four months it has been made probable -
through the work of Joliot in France as well as Fermi and Szilard in
America - that it may become possible to set up a nuclear chain reaction
in a large mass of uranium,by which vast amounts of power and large quant-
ities of new radium-like elements would be generated. Now it appears
almost certain that this could be achieved in the immediate future.

This new phenomenon would also lead to the construction of bombs,
and it is conceivable - though much less certain - that extremely powerful bombs of a new type may thus be constructed. A single bomb of this
type, carried by boat and exploded in a port, might very well destroy
the whole port together with some of the surrounding territory. However,
such bombs might very well prove to be too heavy for transportation by
air.

moderate ....
zechoslovakia,

have some
he group
sible way
a person
fficial

ed of the
rnment action,
ly of uran-

t being car-
tories, by
cts with
s cause,
laboratories

I understand that Germany has actually stopped the sale of uranium
from the Czechoslovakian mines which she has taken over. That she should
have taken such early action might perhaps be understood on the ground
that the son of the German Under-Secretary of State, von Weizsäcker, is
attached to the Kaiser-Wilhelm-Institut in Berlin where some of the
American work on uranium is now being repeated.

Yours very truly,

A. Einstein

(Albert Einstein)

Six years later, almost to the very day, August 6, 1945, an atom bomb exploded with a blinding flash over Japan. The New York *Times* commented: *"It flashed to the minds of men the most spectacular proof of the Einstein Theory of Relativity, which provided the key to the vast treasure house of energy within the atom. . . ."*

But for the people of Hiroshima, it was something different. In a city of 245,000, nearly 100,000 people were killed or doomed by the one bomb! As many more were seriously injured. . . .

$E=mc^2$

"Had I known that the Germans would not succeed in developing an atomic bomb, I would have done nothing for the bomb." ►

Informed of this first use of atomic energy, Einstein sadly shook his head. *"Ach, the world is not yet ready for it,"* he said.

"The release of atomic energy has not created a new problem. It has merely made more urgent the necessity of solving an existing one. . . . A new type of thinking is essential if mankind is to survive a move towards higher levels. . . . At present atomic energy is not a boon to mankind, but a menace. . . ."

Use of atomic energy in the form of a bomb confirmed the scientific theories of Einstein—formulated forty years before. Einstein's entire life represented a fusion of scientific accomplishment together with deep sympathy and respect for people. Primarily he was a man of science. *"Einstein is great,"* states Prof. Arthur H. Compton, Nobel prize winner in physics, *"because he has shown us our world in truer perspective and has helped us to understand a little more clearly how we are related to the universe around us. . . ."*

For a lesser man, these accomplishments would have sufficed. But Einstein's interests were not confined to the scientific world. High among his many social and humanitarian interests was his consistent activity in behalf of the Jewish people, especially the new state of Israel . . . his deep concern for human rights, especially in his adopted country . . . and his all encompassing desire—manifesting itself even in his childhood days—for a peaceful world. . . .

$$R_{ik} = 0$$

Albert Einstein is shown looking over an architect's model of the Albert Einstein College of Medicine, part of Yeshiva University's tribute to him on his seventy-fifth birthday. Pictured from left to right are Dr. Samuel Balkin, president of Yeshiva University; Professor Einstein; Nathaniel L. Goldstein, former New York State Attorney; and Dr. Marcus D. Kogel, dean of the Albert Einstein College of Medicine. ▶

Few testimonials were as gratifying to Einstein as the naming of the Albert Einstein College of Medicine of Yeshiva University in his honor. The college is the first medical school under Jewish auspices to be established in America.

No interest concerned Einstein more than the young state of Israel. From the early days of his life when Prof. Chaim Weizmann introduced him to the need for a Jewish homeland, Einstein had become increasingly devoted to this cause. As Israel's ambassador to this country, Abba Eban, stated: *"Dr. Einstein the scientist and Einstein the Jew represent a perfect harmony. These considerations, added to his deep emotion at the Jewish disaster in Europe . . . explain the ardent zeal with which he advocated and sustained Israel's national revival."*

Einstein and David Ben-Gurion, former prime minister of Israel, meet in Princeton.

Einstein's deep interest in human rights were expressed throughout his life. In America, he often spoke up for full equality for minority groups, particularly the Negro people. *"I believe that whoever tries to think things through honestly will soon recognize how unworthy and even fatal is the traditional bias against Negroes. . . . What can the man of good will do to combat this deeply rooted prejudice? He must have the courage to set an example by words and deed, and must watch lest his children become influenced by racial bias."*

Dr. Horace Mann Bond, president of Lincoln University, is shown awarding an honorary degree to Einstein. Of the many degrees he received from colleges and universities throughout the world, this from a leading Negro university was one of the proudest held.

Time and time again Einstein spoke out in personal letters and written speeches against increasing infringements on the personal liberties of the American people. In many letters, published and unpublished, he cautioned everyone against surrendering any liberty, to *"be prepared for jail and economic ruin, in short, for the sacrifice of his personal welfare in the interest of . . . his country.*

"The strength of the Constitution lies entirely in the determination of each citizen to defend it. Only if every single citizen feels duty bound to do his share in this defense are the constitutional rights secure . . .

"The 'intellectuals' . . . have . . . a particularly strong influence on the formation of public opinion. This is the reason why those who are about to lead us towards an authoritarian government are particularly concerned with intimidating and muzzling that group.

"It is therefore . . . especially important for the intellectuals to do their duty. I see this duty in refusing to cooperate in any undertaking that violates the constitutional rights of the individual. This holds in particular for all inquisitions that are concerned with the private life and the political affiliations of the citizens. . . ."

March 3rd, 1954

Mr. Clark Foreman, Director
Emergency Civil Liberties Committee
421 Seventh Ave.
New York 1, N.Y.

Dear Mr. Foreman:

In the following I am going to answer as best
I can the questions you have put to me in your letter of
February 25th.

1) By academic freedom I understand the right to
search for truth and to publish and teach what one holds to be
true. This right implies also a duty: one must not conceal any
part of what one has recognized to be true. It is evident that
any restriction of academic freedom acts in such a way as to
hamper the dissemination of knowledge among the people and
thereby impedes rational judgment and action.

2) The threat to academic freedom in our time must be
seen in the fact that, because of the alleged external danger
to our country, freedom of t[...] change of opinions,
and freedom of press and ot[...]
croached upon or obstructed [...]
in which people feel their [...]
sequently, more and more [...]
even in their private so[...]
a democratic government[...]

November 30, 1954

Mr. Edward J. Shea
5822 - 16th Ave.
Brooklyn 4, N.Y.

Dear Sir:

thank you for your letter of November 22nd.
A good government resp.constitution is - in my opinion -
one which gives the citizen that _maximum_ amount of liberty and
political rights as is desirable in his own interest.
On the other hand the state has to provide for the
citizen personal security and a certain amount of economic
security. This situation necessitates a compromise between
those two requirements which has to be found according to
circumstances.

Yours very sincerely,

Albert Einstein.

Two of the many letters of advice sent by Einstein. One is to the head of a civil rights committee; the other to a Brooklyn police lieutenant. ▶

There are those who maintain that Einstein was a ready advocate of almost any cause presented to him. Others maintain, however, that a thread of consistency runs through his actions during his entire lifetime. In a message to the Decalogue Society of Lawyers in February, 1954, Einstein declared: *"The existence and validity of human rights are not written in the stars . . . the struggle for human rights is being waged primarily for the freedom of political conviction and discussion. . . . The fear of communism has led to practices which have become incomprehensible to the rest of civilized mankind and expose our country to ridicule. How long shall we tolerate that politicians, hungry for power, try to gain political advantage in such a way?"*

'Refuse to Testify,' Einstein Advises Intellectuals Called In by Congress

By LEONARD BUDER

Dr. Albert Einstein, in a letter made public yesterday, said that every intellectual called before a Congressional investigating committee should refuse to testify, and "must be prepared economic ruin, in sh sacrifice of his person the interest of the cul of his country."

the postscript that it need not be considered confidential.

Reached by telephone at his home in Princeton, N. J., Dr. Einstein confirmed the letter, which

EINSTEIN RALLIES DEFENSE OF RIGHTS

In Replies on Eve of His 75th Birthday He Advocates Resistance to 'Inquisition'

WILLIAM L. LAURENCE

Special to THE NEW YORK TIMES.

RINCETON, N. J., March 13
rof. Albert Einstein today
ed all intellectuals
operate in

Darling Cites Einstein on Testifying

COLUMBUS, O., June 18 (P).—An ousted Ohio State University professor refused today to say whether he was a Communist because "I agree with my fellow physicist, Albert Einstein, that I should refuse to answer tion."

Byron before Activitie ing. He sion

Einstein Again Praises A Witness for Balking

BUFFALO, April 19 (AP)—Dr. Albert Einstein told a Buffalo union leader he did "the right thing" in defying a Congressional subcommittee, the unionist said today.

It was the third time Dr. Einstein was publicly revealed as having individuals

"I call upon the Department of Justice to put a stop to this man Einstein. . . ."— Congressman John Rankin (D.-Miss.), October 25, 1945. ▶

Just as in Germany years ago, Einstein's forthright position on issues of the day earned him sharp criticism from those holding opposite points of view. In 1945 the late Congressman John Rankin of Mississippi condemned Einstein on the floor of Congress, stating: *"It is about time the American people got wise to Einstein. In my opinion he is violating the law and ought to be prosecuted."*

In 1953 Senator Joseph McCarthy stated that anyone who gives advice such as offered by Dr. Einstein *"is himself an enemy of America. . . . It is the same advice that has been given by every Communist lawyer that has ever appeared before our committee."*

Despite these attacks, Einstein continued to express his views on all issues of the day.

100

were intended to be used as a cover—and to obstruct that investigation
ich has been ordered I would denounce

The committee sponsoring the bill
it was not intended and could not
used for that purpose. I believe the
mmittee and I think we should accept
e bill.

Mr. HALLECK. Mr. Speaker, will the
tleman yield?

Mr. COX. I yield to the gentleman
m Indiana.

Mr. HALLECK. Knowing the gentle-
n as I do, I take it that he would be
e of the last men in the House to do
ything that might say to either Kim-
l or Short, "You cannot present your
e before the bar of public opinion
hout regard to whether what you
ow came in a coded message or not."

Mr. COX. If there is going to be an
uiry, I think it should be a full, hon-
, and complete one.

Mr. HALLECK. Can the gentleman
arantee to me those men will be called
d asked by the committee to tell of-
ally what they know?

The SPEAKER. The time of the gen-
man from Georgia has expired.

Mr. COX. Mr. Speaker, I yield 4 min-
s to the gentleman from Mississippi
r. RANKIN].

BILLY MITCHELL—THE ATOMIC BOMB—EINSTEIN AND WAR WITH SPAIN

Mr. RANKIN. Mr. Speaker, one ob-
tion to this bill is it does not go far
ough. I think we should protect our
ret codes, but we should also preserve
e secrets of the know-how, as Presi-
nt Truman calls it, of making the
mic bomb. That is the most impor-
t secret in the world today.

I opposed investigation of the Pearl
rbor incident during the war because
the disturbing effect it might have on
e morale of the country. But the war
over now, and I would be the last man
earth to deny Short or Kimmel a fair
d impartial trial.

But remember that the main witness
nnot be called to testify in the investi-
tion of the Pearl Harbor disaster.
at man is Gen. Billy Mitchell, who was
urt-martialed back in the twenties be-
use he was telling the American peo-
how to build an air force. Pearl Har-
r was lost by the court martial and
nishment and degradation of Billy
tchell, one of the finest and noblest
n America has ever produced.

I understand a bill has passed the Sen-
e to confer upon him a posthumous
dal of Honor; but it has hung fire in
e of the committees of this House. I
nt to serve notice on that committee
w, that if you do not bring it out, we
e going to lay a petition in the well and
ng it out for you; and pass it by a
dslide. We are going to at least let
e world know that Billy Mitchell's
irit marches on, and that we are not
ng to be caught without an air force
ain.

Mr. Speaker, I am serious about the
rets of the atomic bomb. I believe
at we should keep the secret of the
ow-how of making that dangerous
apon at all costs.

I received a letter this morning con-
ning one by Dr. Albert Einstein. In

it is also a card from Dr. Einstein asking for money to carry on the fight for
breaking relations with Spain, which
would probably mean war with that
country.

This morning I received a petition
from a large number of fathers and
mothers in my district asking that the
bodies of their sons, who gave their lives
in this war, be brought home for burial.
The American people do not want another war now, yet here is this man Dr.
Albert Einstein, urging us to break relations, which would likely mean war with
Spain, and probably war with the entire
Spanish-speaking world.

Let me read you what he says:

This campaign will require both work and
money. I am contributing both myself.
You have undoubtedly contributed to other
organizations which are doing splendid work
for the relief of Spanish Republican refugees.
But the American Committee for Spanish
Freedom is an emergency organization—

Then he underscores these words—

It was created solely for the purpose of
working for a break in diplomatic relations
and commercial relations with Nazi-Falange
Spain.

That is the present Spanish Government.

Instead of having our boys come home
this foreign-born agitator would have us
plunge into another European war in
order to further the spread of communism throughout the world.

He tries to frighten us with the sug-
gestion that Spain might attack us some
day with atomic bombs.

What nonsense! A distinguished ad-
miral told us the other day that it would
take England, with all her industry and
ingenuity at least 5 years to make the
machinery with which to make the machinery to manufacture the atomic bomb.
Then how long do you think it would take
backward, impoverished Spain to do it?

It is about time the American people
got wise to Einstein. In my opinion he
is violating the law and ought to be
prosecuted.

Here is a man out demanding that we
break relations with and declare war on
a foreign country that is at peace with
both our country and Great Britain.

Great Britain has never broken relations with Spain because it was Spain's
attitude that enabled Great Britain and
the United States to invade northern
Africa.

Here is a man using the mail to raise
money to propagandize us into breaking
relations with Spain which, as I said,
would mean another war probably
yet these Communists and their
travelers are attacking us for ma
ing a Committee on Un-Ameri
tivities.

I call upon the Department
to put a stop to this man Einste
one else, thus violating the la
Government in order to try to
another war at this time.

We have had enough war.
our boys back home and o
back to peace and prosperity

Mr. MICHENER. Mr. Spe
5 minutes to the gentleman
[Mr. BROWN].

Mr. BROWN of Ohio. Mr.
voted against this rule for

it was before the Committee on Rules
because of the question in my mind relative to two sentences in or portions of
this bill, and it was regarding these two
provisions that I queried the gentleman
from Pennsylvania who opened the de-
bate on this rule.

Instead of answering my queries, he
implied that my questions were prompt-
ed by politics. I say to him and to the
Members of the House if there is any
politics of any kind in this measure, or
in connection with this legislation, it is
not on the minority side of the House or
in my heart or mind.

May I read these two sentences to the
House? I should like for you to read
them with me, if you will. The first is on
page 2, beginning in line 5:

Any material which has been, or purports
to have been—

Get the words "purports to have
been"—

prepared or transmitted in or by the use of
any code, cipher, or cryptographic system of
the United States or any foreign government.

Now please refer to page 3, line 13:

(5) Any information which has been, or
purports to have been, derived from crypt-
analysis of messages transmitted by the
United States.

Under this bill, the divulging of any
such information, whether it is actual
information, or just claimed to be information, is prohibited.

Of course, these restrictions not only
affect Pearl Harbor and the Pearl Harbor
investigation but will affect, control, and
stifle any statement or information
which may ever be given, or be desired to
be given, in the future relative to anything which has happened in our recent
wars.

These two se   broad that
if this law ha   he time
General Wai   ry of
Bataan as i   the
newspapers   es-
sage had   al
MacArthur   nd
he was
sentence
$10,000.

Any er   erah,
who sits   in the
home-tow   age and
begins to   what he
said to M   MacArthur
sent a m   ething
else, coul   d
convict

Active scientist, educator, friend of Israel, defender of human rights . . . Einstein was all of these and more. But it was in the fight for a peaceful world that Einstein demonstrated his most intense concern. *"Taking an active part in the solution of the problems of peace,"* he said, *"is a moral duty which no conscientious man can shirk."*

"The idea of achieving security through national armament is . . . a disastrous illusion. . . . There beckons more and more clearly general annihilation . . . Horrible weapons have been invented capable of destroying in a few seconds huge masses of human beings. . . ."

Ruins of Albert Einstein's former home on Treuchtlinger Strasse in Berlin. All that remain: a few bricks after World War II bombings.

"A leading point of view of all political action should . . . be: What can we do to bring about a peaceful co-existence and even loyal cooperation of the nations?"

"Do you look upon yourself as a German or as a Jew?" Einstein was once asked. *"I look upon myself as a man,"* he answered. *"Nationalism is an infantile disease. It is the measles of mankind."*

"The armament race is the worst method to prevent open conflict. . . . It should not be forgotten that the atomic bomb was made in this country as a preventive measure. . . . A refusal to outlaw the use of the bomb . . . is hardly pardonable."

New York Post

TWO SECTIONS

Rain and cold.

Re-entered as 2d-class matter Nov. 22, 1949, at the Post Office at New York, N. Y., under the act of March 3, 1879

Copyright, 1950, New York Post Corporation

NEW YORK, MONDAY, FEBRUARY 13, 1950

Volume 149,
No. 74.

44 PAGES

Einstein Warns World:

OUTLAW H-BOMB OR PERISH

Story on Page 5

"Our school books glorify war and hide its horrors. They in-culcate hatred in the veins of the children. I would teach peace rather than war. I would inculcate love rather than hate."

It was difficult for friends to believe: but Einstein was getting old. It was difficult to believe because his senses remained as acute as ever . . . his work continued although he retired as an active teacher in 1945 . . . his energy remained enormous . . . his mind receptive to new ideas . . . his memory astounding . . . his sense of humor robust. . . . But on his 75th birthday, a day he would have preferred to ignore, messages and gifts were received from all over the world. Einstein continued to live at his modest Princeton home. The death of his dearly beloved wife in 1938 had been a severe blow to him. It was only in work that Einstein obtained a measure of relief from his loss. After that he lived quietly with his step-daughter, Margot, his secretary, Helen Dukas and his sister, Maja. One of his sons now lived in California, a professor of engineering at the University of California.

Einstein with his sister, Maja. ▲

Mrs. Elsa Einstein, wife of the scientist, who died in 1938. ▶

Einstein meets Prime Minister Jawaharlal Nehru of India. From left to right: Mrs. Indira Gandhi, Nehru's daughter; Einstein; Nehru; and Madam Vijaya Pandit, Indian ambassador to the United States. ▶

Mme. Joliot-Curie, daughter of the discoverers of radium and herself a famous physicist, meets Professor Einstein. ▶

Despite his years, Einstein refused to shut his door to those who needed his advice and counsel. *"I speak to everyone in the same way,"* he said, *"whether he is the garbage man or the president of the university."* And he did. Whether it was a conference with a prime minister or . . .

110

. . . whether walking down the streets of Princeton . . . relaxing with friends . . . or exchanging views on a geometry problem with a school girl, Einstein treated all people the same . . . with respect and a desire to be of service. . . .

▲ Einstein in a rumble seat. Intimate picture of Dr. Einstein, his sister, Maja, and Dr. Gustav Bucky and family.

Always a lover of sailing, Einstein is shown in a typical informal pose. ▶

When a school girl wrote to Einstein for help in her geometry work, he sent his answer. ▼

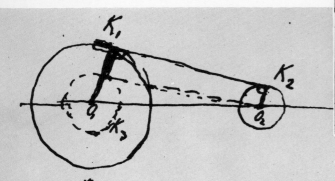

he radius of K_3 is the difference $r_3 = r_1 - r_2$.

The tangent $O_2 \to K_3$ is $\parallel$ to the tangent on K_1 and K_2 and can be easily constructed. This gives the solution.

A. E.

The huge Riverside Church in New York included a statue of only one living person among its carvings of the world's greatest scholars: Einstein. When asked how it felt to find himself "among the saints," Einstein replied: *I am proud of the honor, not on my account, but because I am a Jew.*

114

But for the seventy-six-year-old scientist—*time* which he had

spent a lifetime studying—was running out. One day the world

learned that one of its greatest sons was no more. . . .

116

March 14, 1879—April 18, 1955

New York World-Telegram
and The Sun

7TH SPORTS
BASEBALL
RACE RESULTS
WALL ST.

NEW YORK, MONDAY, APRIL 18, 1955. FIVE CENTS

ALBERT EINSTEIN DIES AT 76

Story on Page 1, Main Section

WARM
Warm, cloudy Monday, high near 60°; low during night 40°. Cooler, showers Tuesday.

VOL. 116—No. 92

CINCINNATI TIMES-STAR

STATE EDITION
LATEST SCRATCHES

Cincinnati's Home-Owned Newspaper—Founded 1840
MONDAY, APRIL 18, 1955   30 Pages

Phone CH 1700   5c See above 30c

Albert Einstein, Noted Scientist, Dies

Acclaimed

SHOWERS
Cloudy with occasional showers today, tonight and Tuesday. High today, low 70s. Low tonight, mid-40s. High Tuesday near 70.

CHICAGO DAILY NEWS
An Independent Newspaper

80TH YEAR—91   Tel. DEarborn 2-1111   MONDAY, APRIL 18, 1955   44 PAGES   **5¢**

BLUE STREAK

PARTY LINE REVERSED
Drop the Wrench And Get a Wench, Ivan! It's OK Now
Cupid Clobbers Class Struggle Behind the Iron Curtain
BY WILLIAM McGAFFIN
Daily News Foreign Service
NEW YORK — They're taking a new line on love behind the Iron Curtain.

EINSTEIN DEAD
Noted Scientist Father of Atom Age

IN PHILADELPHIA
NEARLY EVERYBODY READS
THE BULLETIN

The Evening Bulletin   NIGHT EXTRA

WITH SUNDAY MORNING EDITION

PHILADELPHIA, MONDAY, APRIL 18, 1955   FIVE CENTS

109th YEAR, No. 7

Albert Einstein Dies in Princeton at 76

29 States Open   Brief Pause for Informal Search at Airport

Pittsburgh Post-Gazette

One of America's Great Newspapers

BASE BALL   **LATE NEWS**

WEATHER: Warm; scattered thundershowers.   TUESDAY MORNING, APRIL 19, 1955   Telephone ATlantic 1-6100   FIVE CENTS

VOL. 28—NO. 225   In Three Sections

ALBERT EINSTEIN DIES AT 76

WEATHER
Partly cloudy, warmer, high 68 Monday, cloudy tonight, Tuesday. Cloudy Tuesday afternoon. Low tonight 50.

Vol. 91—No. 1

THE EVENING SUN   **5 STAR**

BALTIMORE, MONDAY, APRIL 18, 1955   48 Pages   5 Cents

Afro-Asian Parley Hears Reds Denounced
EINSTEIN DIES AT PRINCETON

"No other man contributed so much to the vast expansion of twentieth-century knowledge."
—DWIGHT D. EISENHOWER
President of the United States

"The great scientist of our age, he was truly a seeker after truth who would not compromise with evil or untruth."
—JAWAHARLAL NEHRU
Prime Minister of India

"A powerful searchlight of the human mind, piercing by its rays the darkness of the unknown, has suddenly been extinguished. The world has lost its foremost genius and the Jewish people its most illustrious son in the present generation."
—MOISHE SHARETT
Prime Minister of Israel

"The world and the country have suffered a great loss."
—HARRY S. TRUMAN
former President of the United States

"He was one of the greats of all ages. For all scientists and most men, this is a day of mourning."
—J. ROBERT OPPENHEIMER
Director of the Institute of Advanced
Study, Princeton, N. J.

"This one man changed human thinking about the world as only Newton and Darwin changed it."
—*New York Times*

120

"The world has lost an illustrious scientist, a great and brave mind and a fighter for human rights. The Jewish people have lost the brightest jewel in their crown."

—MRS. VERA WEIZMANN
widow of the late Israeli President

"Dr. Einstein was one of the obviously good men. He initiated some of the greatest revolutions of thinking in all science."

—DR. HAROLD C. UREY
Institute of Nuclear Studies
University of Chicago

"A great transformer of natural science has been lost."
—Pravda
Moscow, U.S.S.R.

"There will be no finer monument to the memory of this great man than universal peace and the peaceful uses of his scientific discoveries."

—The Advance
Amalgamated Clothing Workers of America

"With the passing of Dr. Albert Einstein, the world has lost its greatest scientific mind, the human race one of its most ethical and inspiring personalities, the Jewish people one of its most loyal sons."

—DR. SAMUEL BELKIN
President, Yeshiva University

"One cannot contemplate without astonishment and admiration work at once so profound and so powerfully original achieved in a few years."

—PRINCE LOUIS DE BROGLIE
permanent secretary of the
French Academy of Science

121

"No tribute can be adequate. His death is a great loss
to science, and a greater loss to the world of a good and
kindly man."

—Prof. A. M. Low
president of the British Institute
of Engineering Technology

"The contributions which Dr. Einstein made to man's
understanding of nature are beyond assessment in our
day. Only future generations will be competent to grasp
their full significance."

—Dr. Harold W. Dodds
president of Princeton University

"Mankind has lost its finest son, whose mind reached
out to the ends of the universe but whose heart over-
flowed with concern for the peace of the world and the
well-being, not of humanity as an abstraction, but of
ordinary men and women everywhere."

—Dr. Israel Goldstein
president of the American Jewish Congress

"He was a great citizen of the world and one of the
true giants of this age."

—Senator Herbert H. Lehman

"The memory of his noble personality will always remain a fresh source of inspiration and strength to those
of us who were happy enough to become personally
acquainted with him."

—Niels Bohr
Danish atomic scientist

"I would be unable to picture science without him.
His spirit permeates it. He makes part of my thinking
and outlook."

—Albert Szent-Gyorgy
Nobel Laureate in Medicine and Physiology

for such steps; question we have to ask ourselves is: What steps can be taken to prevent a military contest of which the issue must be disastrous to all parties?

Most of us are not neutral in feeling, but, as human beings, we have to remember that, if the issues between East and West are to be decided in any manner that can give any possible satisfaction to anybody, whether Communist or anti Communist, whether Asian or European or American, whether white or black, then these issues must not be decided by war. We should wish this to be understood, both in the East and in the West.

In view of the fact that in any future world war nuclear weapons will certainly be employed, and that such weapons threaten the continued existence of mankind, we urge the governments of the world to realize and to acknowledge publicly, that their purpose cannot be furthered by a world war, and we urge them, consequently, to find peaceful means for the settlement of all matters of dispute between them."

Lord Bertrand Russell reading the statement of prominent scientists. ▶

◀ From statement, of scientists, urging peaceful means of settling world disputes.

Three months after Einstein's death, his friend Lord Bertrand Russell in England made public a statement sponsored by Einstein and a number of other prominent scientists throughout the world. It was the last public statement of Albert Einstein. Perhaps it was in reference to this that he once said: *"I am waiting for the critical moment to come. Then I will shout with all the strength left in me. . . ."*

"There is no higher religion than human service.

To work for the common good is the greatest creed."

PICTORIAL ACKNOWLEDGMENTS

The author gratefully thanks and extends credit to the many sources—some of which are listed below—that contributed pictorial and other matter for this volume. Although it is impossible to give proper recognition to all such sources, the following were most helpful:

Fred Stein: cover portrait.

Lotte Jacobi: pages 2, 15, 20, 29, 41 (bottom), 55, 73, 109 (bottom), 113 (middle), 127.

Brown Brothers: pages 8 (bottom), 17 (bottom), 19, 39, 43 (top), 47, 65, 67.

Underwood and Underwood: pages 23, 25 (bottom), 31, 35, 41 (top), 45, 53, 54, 56, 57, 59, 62, 82.

International News Photos: pages 11, 37, 38, 75, 78, 79, 81, 87, 95.

United Press Pictures: pages 64, 71, 77, 89, 97 (bottom), 109 (top), 111, 113.

Wide World: pages 79 (top and bottom), 83, 103, 107, 117, 123, 125.

New York Public Library: pages 8 (top), 9, 27, 49, 51, 101.

Albert Einstein College of Medicine: page 91.

Bettmann Archives: page 17 (top).

Free Lance Photographers (FPG): pages 33, 61, 80 (middle).

The Riverside Church: page 115.

Library of Congress: pages 63, 68, 69.

Mr. Alexander Sacks: page 106.

Dr. Thomas Bucky: page 113 (top).

Alexander Archer: page 93.